OCTOPUSES

ELIZABETH THOMAS

Published in the United States of America by Cherry Lake Publishing
Ann Arbor, Michigan
www.cherrylakepublishing.com

Consultants: Dominique A. Didier, PhD, Associate Professor, Department of Biology, Millersville University;
Marla Conn, ReadAbility, Inc.
Book design: Sleeping Bear Press

Photo Credits: ©Thierry Duran/Shutterstock Images, cover, 1; ©Mikhail Blajenov/Dreamstime.com, 5; ©Sergey Popov
V/Shutterstock Images, 6; ©PlanctonVideo/iStockphoto, 7; ©Brian Gratwicke/http://www.flickr.com/ CC-BY-2.0, 9;
©Dorling Kindersley RF/Thinkstock, 11; ©lecates/http://www.flickr.com/ CC-BY-2.0, 12; ©Dario Sabljak/Shutterstock
Images, 13; ©Silke Baron/http://www.flickr.com/ CC-BY-2.0, 15; ©Shane Gross/Shutterstock Images, 16; ©Vittorio
Bruno/Shutterstock Images, 19, 27; ©Andreas Altenburger/Shutterstock Images, 21; ©Matt Wilson/Jay Clark, NOAA
NMFS AFSC./http://www.flickr.com/ CC-BY-2.0, 22; ©kangarooarts/Shutterstock Images, 25; ©Serban Enache/
Dreamstime.com, 26; ©DanBrandenburg/iStockphoto, 28

Library of Congress Cataloging-in-Publication Data

Thomas, Elizabeth, 1953- author.
Octopuses / Elizabeth Thomas.
     pages cm. — (Exploring our oceans)
   Summary: "Introduces facts about octopus, including physical features, habitat, life cycle, food,
and threats to these ocean creatures. Photos, captions, and keywords supplement the narrative of
this informational text"— Provided by publisher.
   Audience: 8-12.
   Audience: Grades 4 to 6.
   Includes bibliographical references and index.
   ISBN 978-1-62431-601-2 (hardcover) — ISBN 978-1-62431-613-5 (pbk) —
   ISBN 978-1-62431-625-8 (pdf) — ISBN 978-1-62431-637-1 (ebook)
   1. Octopuses—Juvenile literature. I. Title.

QL430.3.O2T47 2014
594.56—dc23   2013041379

Cherry Lake Publishing would like to acknowledge the work of
The Partnership for 21st Century Skills. Please visit *www.p21.org*
for more information.

Printed in the United States of America
Corporate Graphics Inc.
January 2014

ABOUT THE AUTHOR

Elizabeth Thomas has written and edited books for children for many years. She has a master's
degree in writing for children and young adults from Hamline University in St. Paul, Minnesota.
She lives on Cape Cod, Massachusetts. She spends her summers scanning the shores and tide
pools for octopuses.

TABLE OF CONTENTS

CHAPTER 1

THE AMAZING OCTOPUS

Swimming in the ocean the hungry sperm whale hunts for food. The octopus senses the predator overhead and hides itself. The whale continues swimming in search of food. When a second sperm whale notices the octopus, the eight-armed creature releases its black ink, blocking the whale's vision.

There are more than 200 species of octopuses. They come in many different sizes. The smallest octopus lives in the Indian Ocean. It measures only about 1 inch (2.54 cm) across. The giant Pacific octopus can weigh as much as

110 pounds (50 kg) and can measure more than 20 feet (6 m) across. Octopuses can be found along the coastlines and on the floors of tropical and semitropical oceans around the world.

The giant octopus has been trained to open jars and solve mazes, while being studied in labs.

Do you think this octopus will be able to fit inside this jar?

Octopuses don't have a hard outer shell to protect them. Many of them create homes in an opening in a rock or in a section of a coral reef. Even the largest octopuses can squeeze their bodies into an opening the size of an orange. They might dig themselves a hole in the sand for protection. Octopuses have even built homes out of empty coconut shells. They also make their home in empty bottles and cans. Octopuses will often collect shells or rocks and put them outside the opening of their home. These help to hide their den from predators and add more protection.

This octopus floats near the surface in tropical or temperate waters.

LOOK AGAIN

LOOK CLOSELY AT THIS PHOTOGRAPH. DOES THIS OCTOPUS REMIND YOU OF ANOTHER ANIMAL? WHERE HAVE YOU SEEN AN OCTOPUS?

CHAPTER 2

Now You See It

The word *octopus* comes from an ancient Greek word that means "eight-footed." An octopus has no bones. This allows it to squeeze into tiny crevices to escape predators. Its eight arms are attached directly to its head. Many cartoonists draw octopuses with large, round heads. In real life, the large round thing is a **mantle** that holds organs, an ink sac, and the brain. An octopus's head is behind its large eyes. Octopuses have not one, not two, but three hearts. Two of these hearts pump blood to the creature's gills, and the third heart pumps blood to rest of the octopus's body. Octopuses have very large brains and each arm has its own spinal cord.

Each tentacle has two rows of suction cups with about 250 suckers on each arm.

The only shell-like part of an octopus is its hard, sharp, parrot-like beak. The beak is located on the bottom of the octopus's head, right in the center where the arms join the head. It is used to crush the shells of crabs, lobsters, and other food. Inside the beak is a raspy tongue, called a **radula**. The radula is used for getting through a tough shell. It is also used to tear off food and pull it into the octopus's mouth.

The octopus has two eyes, one on either side of its head. Although octopuses are invertebrates, their eyes are very similar to human eyes. Octopuses have excellent eyesight and can see as far away as 8 feet (2.4 m). This helps them find their prey.

GO DEEPER

WHY DO YOU THINK AN OCTOPUS HAS SO MANY WAYS OF DEFENDING ITSELF? ARE THERE DEFENSES MORE EFFECTIVE THAN THE ONES OF AN OCTOPUS?

BODY DIAGRAM

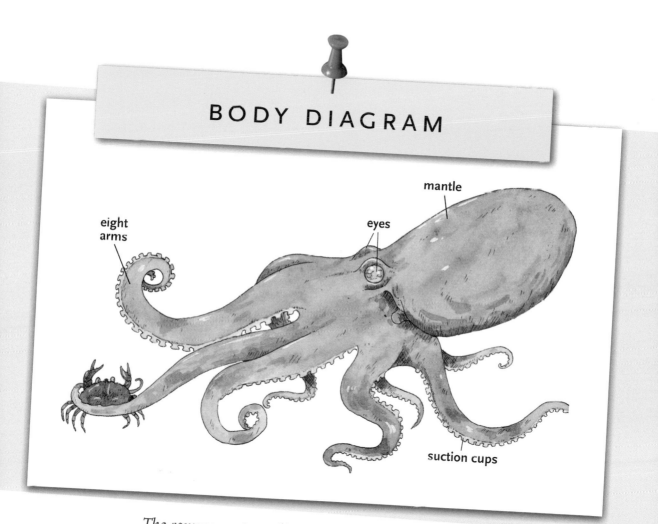

mantle

eyes

eight arms

suction cups

The common octopus lives one to two years in the wild.

Each suction cup is surrounded by muscles.

The eight arms of an octopus are called **tentacles**. Underneath each tentacle are two rows of **suction cups**. The suction cups enable the octopus to hold on to slippery food, taste things, and move along the ocean rocks. The tentacles are long and strong, and can twist and coil in any direction. They are used to do many things. They help the octopus catch its food, move around the bottom of the ocean, build its den, and protect itself.

These tentacles are wonderful tools with some surprising features. For example, they can save an octopus's life. If a tentacle is caught by a predator, the octopus can detach it and escape. Eventually, a new tentacle will grow back. If a tentacle gets separated from an octopus and it comes across some food, the tentacle has been known to pass the food back to where the head used to be!

Another tool that the octopus uses to protect itself and send a signal to others is its skin. If it needs to blend in more to hide from predators, the octopus can actually change color. Octopus skin is covered with cells that have **pigment**. Each cell contains yellow, red, brown, or black pigment. Its skin can also change patterns. This **camouflage** helps the octopus blend into its surroundings. It can match a stand of algae, show stripes to scare off competitors, or display dots to look like a coral reef. ⚓

Do you see the octopus in this photograph?

CATCHING PREY

Octopuses are predators—they eat other sea animals. They live on shelled animals such as crabs, lobsters, clams, and scallops. They also eat fish and sometimes even other octopuses! Most octopuses hunt at night.

The octopus uses its sharp senses to find food. When an octopus sees something it wants to eat, it has several different methods of catching its prey. For a surprise attack, the octopus hides among the rocks and leaps out, catching the prey with its long tentacles. The suction cups on the tentacles latch onto to the prey, making escape almost impossible. The sensitive suction cups also smell and taste, to see if what they are holding will be good to eat. If it is, the octopus will bite it with its beak, injecting it with a toxin that stuns it. The octopus often gathers several items of food under its arms and carries the food back to its den. There the octopus can eat and be safe from its own predators.

This octopus used its parrot-like beak to break the crab's shell.
Its beak is made of the same material as fingernails.

Octopus hunt for food on the ocean floor.

LOOK AGAIN

LOOK CLOSELY AT THIS PHOTOGRAPH. WHAT METHOD IS THE OCTOPUS USING TO HUNT ITS PREY?

Another way of catching prey is to go hunting. When an octopus finds a likely spot to hunt on the ocean floor, it will spread out its body. Then it will use its tentacles to poke into holes and pull out food. The animals cannot escape because the octopus is covering them like a parachute.

If its meal does not have a shell, the octopus will tear off pieces with its beak. If the food does have a hard shell, the octopus will drill a hole through the shell. Then it will inject the food with saliva that paralyzes the prey. The saliva also causes the prey to become mushy. Using its toothed tongue, the octopus scrapes the meat out of the shell.

One Hundred Thousand Eggs

Octopuses do not spend their lives living in families or large colonies with other octopuses. But once in their lifetime, if they have the opportunity, they will mate.

When a male and female octopus start to mate, they face each other. They begin by reaching out with their tentacles. Often they will change colors, and their skin texture turns pebbly. The ritual can look violent, with thrashing tentacles and beak thrusts. Sometimes the female will even eat her mate.

This Octopus Macropus *has the nickname white-spotted or grass octopus.*

The male octopus uses a special arm, called a **hectocotylus**, to place packages of sperm inside the female. After mating, the male loses interest in eating and dies.

The female finds herself a safe den. She can lay up to 100,000 eggs. She uses sticky mucus to hang the eggs in long clusters on the walls and ceiling of the den. She then curls up and takes care of the eggs. It is a full-time job. She keeps other animals from coming into the den. She cleans the eggs and keeps them free of algae or any dirt. She sprays them with water to give them oxygen. During this time, she does not eat very much.

Depending on the species, the eggs could take four to six weeks or up to six months to hatch. When the baby octopuses are ready to hatch, the female showers them with water, which helps them break free of their egg sacs. A short time after the eggs have hatched, the female octopus dies.

*A baby octopus in the water
could be mistaken for a spider!*

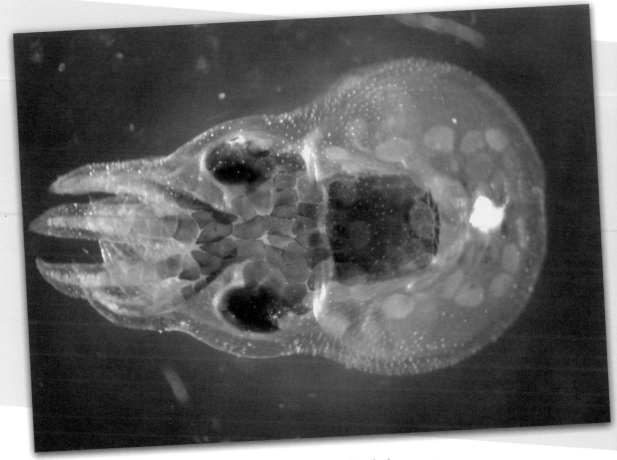

Adult octopuses do not care for their young.

The tiny hatchlings, which are the size of fleas, have to take care of themselves. They are born knowing how to propel themselves around, change colors, and squirt ink.

They immediately float to the surface and disguise themselves among the clouds of **plankton**. They eat whatever they can fit into their tiny mouths. Many of them are eaten by other sea creatures. After a few weeks, they grow big enough to sink to the ocean floor and find homes.

Depending on the species of octopus, they can live anywhere from six months to three years. The average age of an octopus is one year.

THINK ABOUT IT

WHAT WERE THE SURPRISING FACTS YOU LEARNED FROM THIS CHAPTER? DISCUSS THESE WITH A FRIEND OR CLASSMATE.

A Smart Creature

At every stage of their lives, octopuses are a source of food for many different animals. These include fish such as moray eels and orange roughy, albatross, seals, and sperm whales. Almost anything that is big enough to eat an octopus will try to do it.

People have also eaten octopuses since ancient times. Octopus meat is considered a delicacy and is eaten by human beings all over the world. Octopus fisheries trap thousands of octopuses a year. They are caught by using plastic pots that the octopuses mistake for safe hiding places.

[21ST CENTURY SKILLS LIBRARY]

Octopuses will mistake a fisherman's trap for a safe hiding place.

Known to be the most intelligent of all invertebrates, octopuses can be a problem for commercial fishermen. Octopuses have figured out how to open the traps set for fish or crabs. And octopuses have excellent memories. They remember where the traps are located, and return over and over to get a free meal!

Octopuses can change color to match their surroundings.

Because octopuses have the misfortune of being delicious to so many species, they have developed clever ways to avoid capture. One of their first lines of defense when they feel threatened is to hide themselves in plain sight. Remember, they are able to change the color and pattern of their skin to blend instantly into whatever background is available.

Attackers are tricked by the black ink cloud.

If the octopus is discovered, it will squirt a cloud of ink at the perceived threat. The ink cloud actually resembles an octopus. It also contains a scent that dulls the senses of the attacker, making it harder to find the octopus. Hidden by the dark cloud, the octopus can shoot water through its body and swim away quickly. It can then squeeze its boneless body into a tiny opening in a rock where the attacker cannot follow.

A rubber duck makes a good octopus toy.

LOOK AGAIN

LOOK CLOSELY AT THIS PHOTO. DO YOU KNOW WHY OCTOPUSES LIVING IN AQUARIUMS ARE GIVEN TO TOYS TO PLAY WITH?

If all else fails, the octopus can detach one of its tentacles. The tentacle will wriggle away and distract the attacker while the octopus makes its escape. Eventually, the octopus can grow a new tentacle. This process is called **regeneration**.

It is very difficult to keep octopuses as pets. They are excellent escape artists and will find a way to get out of their aquariums. They are so strong that they can lift off a lid that has been weighed down with two cinder blocks.

Because octopuses are so smart, aquarium caregivers often provide octopuses with toys to keep them from being bored and trying to escape. They also give them their food in jars. After the octopus has unscrewed the jar lid and eaten the food, it will sometimes screw the lid back on.

THINK ABOUT IT

- In chapter 2, you learned about how an octopus is able to camouflage itself by changing the color of its skin. Learn about another animal that can camouflage itself by changing the color of its skin.

- Can you think of another creature that has eight arms? How does its hunting methods differ from those of an octopus?

- In chapter 4 you learned that an octopus lays many eggs. What other animals can you think of that produce many offspring? What other animals have to survive without parental guidance and protection when they are born?

LEARN MORE

FURTHER READING

Greenberg, Nicki. *It's True! An Octopus Has Deadly Spit*. New York: Annick Press, 2007.

Markert, Jenny. *Octopuses*. Mankato, MN: The Child's World, 2008.

Shea, Therese. *The Bizarre Life Cycle of an Octopus*. New York: Gareth Stevens Publishing, 2013.

WEB SITES

A–Z Animals: Octopus
http://a-z-animals.com/animals/octopus
This Web site includes many photos of octopuses, animal quizzes and links to animal blogs.

National Geographic—Octopuses
http://kids.nationalgeographic.com/kids/animals/creaturefeature/octopuses
Read fun facts, see interesting photos, and look at a map of where octopuses live.

GLOSSARY

camouflage (KAM-uh-flahj) an animal's natural coloring that enables it to blend in with its surroundings

hectocotylus (hek-toh-KOT-uh-luss) a modified arm used by male octopuses to transfer sperm to the female

invertebrates (in-VUR-tuh-brits) animals without a backbone

mantle (MAN-tuhl) an outer or enclosing layer of tissue

pigment (pig-muhnt) a substance in the cells of plants or animals that provides color

plankton (PLANGK-tuhn) aquatic plants and animals that are usually small and that drift in the water

radula (RA-juh-luh) a tonguelike structure with raspy teeth used for scraping food particles off a surface and drawing them into the mouth

regeneration (re-jen-uh-RAY-shun) the act of forming new animal or plant tissue

sperm (SPURM) male reproductive cell

suction cups (SUK-chun KUPS) soft round cups that cling to a surface when they are flattened against it; octopuses have suction cups on the undersides of their tentacles

tentacles (TEN-tuh-kuhlz) slender, flexible limbs or appendages in an animal, used for grasping or moving around, or containing sense organs

INDEX